HEART

BUILDING A GREAT BRAND IN THE DIGITAL AGE

Dan Pestretto

Copyright © 2014 **Dan Pestretto**
All rights reserved.

ISBN: **1501052276**
ISBN 13: **9781501052279**
LCCN**: 2014915860**

Produced by L'Ouverture Independent
Publishing New York
610 W 174 Street
Manhattan, NY, 10033

Prepress Production
 Dr. Margret Brito, PhD

BISAC:
Business Economics/Development/
Business Development

HeartBranding.net

Table of Contents

Overture

Chapter 1: It Started with a Birch Tree…

Chapter 2: Principles of Heart

Chapter 3: Branding from the Inside Out

Chapter 4: Own Your Intelligence

Chapter 5: The Coming of Age of the Brand

Chapter 6: Evolution of the Brand in the Digital Age

Chapter 7: Believe in What You Sell: A Heart-Centered Sales Process

Chapter 8: The Meditation Garden

Chapter 9: The (He)art of Branding

Chapter 10: Failure As a Rite of Passage

Chapter 11: Leadership and the Praxis of Heart-Centered Branding

Chapter 12: The Science of Branding

Chapter 13: Building Your Brand in the Trenches

Chapter 14: We Love Gardening, and It Shows!

Chapter 15: Maintaining Your Brand's Integrity

A Final Word

Acknowledgments

First off, I'd like to thank Dr. Margaret Brito for her help in this work's production. Her heart was in it from the beginning.

Writing a book is never easy, but starting with a blank piece of paper and an open mind is something I learned from Michael E. Gerber in the Dreaming Room. Well, we began with a blank piece of paper and open minds, plus, as Maggie so often told me, a ridiculously short amount of time to put this book together. Was it the structure, the pressure, the subject, or all three that made this book appeal to her? I'm not sure. I just know that it wouldn't be the book it is today without her help.

I express my gratitude to my friends, family, and clients who were incredibly understanding of my absence and preoccupation during the writing of this book.

Most of all, I want to thank my wife, who has been so supportive through all of this. I never would have been able to attempt any of this—the book, a new company, and all the trials that go with it—without her support and encouragement. She not only put up with my reading to her those parts of the book that were difficult to write, but she listened and helped me make them better. She has many superpowers, but her greatest one is patience.

Dedication

I dedicate this book to people struggling in business. Finding what you love isn't as hard as loving what you do. If you can create value, discover meaning, and find purpose in serving others, you're on your way to building a great brand in this digital age.

OVERTURE

You've dared to risk everything in pursuit of your dream. You've taken the plunge. You're an entrepreneur, the founder of your own dynasty. You know without any doubt you're following your star.

You're in a fruitful dimension, in which there is the height of your dream, the depth of your integrity, the breadth of your commitment to your values, a long past behind you in which you've garnered your hard-won experience, and a long future ahead in which you'll weave all you've got into a new creation.

But it's a difficult road because it's truly your path. You know you're on the right path when the way becomes so hard you wonder if you'll make it. The more lofty your dream, the more difficult will be your path, because you demand more of yourself and life demands more of you. The greater your vision of your destiny, the more difficult the way. So stand up!

Success doesn't mean you don't experience challenges and problems. Indeed, success will surely bring you more challenges than you had before, for problems and their solutions have always been the impetus for invention, innovation, and progress. See these challenges as increased opportunities for gaining new knowledge and coming to know what you're truly made of. Embrace them!

We're made to think large thoughts and nurture great visions. We're built to be more than we were schooled to believe we can be. So when you're in the trenches, shovel in hand, building your brand block by painful block, remember you're there because you're worthy of your dream.

So stand up and let the light of your new creation illumine and enlighten all around you. Let this business you've brought into being be one of the myriad of beacons that light humanity's way into our future. Stand up!

For you're in business to make your unique and extraordinary contribution to humanity and do something that's never been done before.

CHAPTER 1
IT STARTED WITH A BIRCH TREE...

I was born into a family business. The business, a small landscape nursery, was a big part of our lives. At least it was for me. I wouldn't be lying if I said I was born and raised to inherit my father's business.

My family moved from the city to open land when I was three years old, and my father planted a nursery from stock he ordered from the *American Nurseryman Magazine*. Every month, this glossy black-and-white magazine arrived in the mail, its cover graced by a stately tree. Large wholesale nurseries advertised in the back of the magazine, and my dad chose what he wanted from those ads. When the trees arrived, I excitedly accompanied him to the train station to pick up the boxes that contained the trees.

I loved to spend time with my dad in our nursery after dinner. Once a month or so, he cultivated the nursery using a Gravely rototiller.

That machine was rugged. It was old back then, and I can remember seeing it in my father's barn twenty years later. We called it a *cultivator*.

It turned over the soil as my father ran it through every row of plants in the nursery, while he walked one row behind it. My dad wore big, brown working boots and walked with his toes pointed outward. I'd follow, stepping into his footprints exactly as he made them.

When he reached the end of a row, he'd lift the front of the machine and make a U-turn into the next row. While its blades were suspended in the air, the machine made a shrill whirring noise as it sped up, and I, too, sped up to a run to keep up with my dad.

I loved those times. I loved the nursery. Even then, when I was so little, I knew growing up there was perfect.

One day, some birch trees arrived in a box at the station. I liked birch trees. There was one next to our house, a gorgeous clump paper birch that swept upward from five stems at its base. Its white peeling bark was fascinating and looked beautiful against our gray house. One of the new birch trees was beautiful like that, and I openly admired it. When my dad saw how much I liked the tree, he gave it to me. It was of no real use to me except that he'd given it to me and told me that, when he sold it, all the money he got from it would be mine.

A few years later, he sold it for a hundred dollars! One hundred dollars in the 1960s was a fortune to a nine-year-old boy. From that point on, I was hooked. I knew I'd be involved in business for the rest of my life.

My dad also owned a landscaping business and pulled plants from the nursery for his jobs and to sell to the public. He worked hard out in people's yards and on commercial projects six days a week.

Every morning at 6:45 a.m. he walked across the street to meet the men that came out to work with him. Every evening at 4:30 p.m., my brother, my sister, and I sat on the stoop of our house's front door, waiting for him to come back to the barn. He came back every day at the same time—4:30 p.m. When we saw him, we'd run down our driveway to meet him and help him empty his pant cuffs on the front stoop. Then at 5:15, my mom would have dinner on the table. At 5:25, the radio would announce the next day's weather, and no one could talk during those next five minutes. It was the same thing every day, five days a week.

On Saturdays, my dad went to work at 6:45 a.m. and came back at noon. He and his men worked forty-five hours a week, every week, during the season, which ran from April 1 through Thanksgiving. My dad worked all the time. When he wasn't out on jobs, he was in the barn repairing equipment or in the nursery tending to the plants.

The winters were my favorite times. That was when I got to go with my dad when he went out plowing snow. During snowstorms we got to ride together and talk, and I got to know him. Those were great times. I loved to work, too, and I really liked being with him in the truck.

Giving me that tree was a very smart thing for my father to do, and I'm thankful he did it. It gave me a goal, a future I could envision. My father had followed in his father's footsteps, and nothing would have pleased him more than if I had done the same. But there came a time when I no longer wanted to walk in anybody's footsteps. I wanted to chart my own path. So after graduating from the University of Connecticut with a degree in horticulture, I worked for my dad a bit and then went off to see the world…

I ended up in Paris. I thought I'd spend a month or two there—or maybe six, if I really liked it. I wound up staying four years, and it was glorious.

For a young American, being in Paris was as good as one might imagine. I was in my late twenties, and my life was about girls and fun. But Paris was also an education. I worked as a bartender and learned about wine and people. I worked in some of the best restaurants and learned about food and entertaining. I started a theater group with some seed money I got from a Parisian banker friend of mine.

Inevitably, during my work and travels, someone would hear of my background in horticulture and I'd find myself helping out in people's gardens. But my main occupation and most of the money I earned was from singing. Horticulture was something nice to do while the sun shone, and it gave me opportunities to get to know people better than if I only sang to them at night. It was a great life, and I loved it. Living in Paris as an American taught me a lot about people and a lot about myself.

Parisians loved American music. At that time in the 1980s, they loved jazz. I sang jazz and Broadway tunes in bars and hotels, and I worked in theaters. In order to survive, one had to be good at what one was doing. I got good, and I survived there for four years. I've carried the confidence that experience gave me throughout my life.

Part of the confidence I gained came from the work I did. People tend to admire singers more than they do landscapers. When I realized I could be really good at singing, I also recognized I could be really good at other things as well. I still carry this confidence with me when I'm leading organizations or selling services to some of the richest, most accomplished people in the world.

As a singer, if your heart isn't in your work, you ain't working. People can feel it. People pay to feel it. They want to feel what you're feeling, what the composer felt when he or she wrote the lyrics and composed the tune. Pretty singing isn't what they come to hear. They come to be moved. Moved by your emotions. Your pain. Your joy. Your sadness. Your heart.

CHAPTER 2
PRINCIPLES OF HEART

Heart

Emotional and intellectual energy. Intensity revealed and demonstrated in your work. Bold and ballsy risk taking. Integrity. Truth. Bravery. Honesty.

Heart-Centered Action

Action infused with the emotional and intellectual energy of heart. Heart-centered action emerges from the entrepreneur's intelligence and creative energy. The expression of your core values in your conversation and your work.

Heart-Centered Work

Work performed with the recognition of the intrinsic value of people. Inspired work filled with feeling, emotion and passion. Work filled with warmth, energy, vitality, and spirit.

Work done for the purpose of making a profit as well as empowering people and improving communities. The means by which you, the entrepreneur, come to understand and develop your place in your community.

Heart-Centered Entrepreneurship

The highest expression of business. The act of bringing something into the world that hadn't been there before and that's singularly beneficial to the world. A praxis that ensures a company fulfills the desires of its employees, its customers, and its community better than any of its competitors, better than anyone has done before, and at higher profit margins.

Heart-Centered Leadership

Leadership that guides a company to its better, truer self. Spontaneous, authentic, and real. Leading as an act of love for your business, your employees, and the community you serve.

Heart is a modus operandi that marks a business as extraordinary and shoots it way ahead of its competition.

When you perform your work with heart, your conversation is authentic and your actions are intrinsically motivated.

When you do business with heart, your clients instantly recognize this as such. You don't have to tell them—they know it.

When, as an entrepreneur, you contemplate your business with heart, you're able to envision and achieve the extraordinary.

CHAPTER 3
BRANDING FROM THE INSIDE OUT

Why are you in business? Why does your company exist? Why do you get up and do what you do every day? Why should anyone care?

The answers to these questions are at the heart of your business and are the reason for being, the cause or motivation of your company.

When I ask people why they're in business, the most common answer I hear is, "To make living." But that answer has to do with results. It's not about why. *Why* has to do with what you believe about yourself, your community, and the contribution you believe you can make to people's lives.

Most of us work because we have to, but what we choose to do has its roots in *why*. When I ask business owners what they believe about their fields—whether the field be HVAC, landscaping, consulting, electrical, or alternative energy—their answers, most of the time, initiate our exploration into the *why* of their businesses.

Then when I ask them to describe their business models and explain how they're different, we get deeper into the *why*.

As I probe a company, as I learn about its services and how it solves people's problems, as I talk about how it meets their needs or fulfills their desires, its *why* comes more and more clearly into view.

Entrepreneurs go into business for a wide variety of reasons, but those who have a shot at building a great brand go into business in fields they know well and perform tasks they're good at. They feel inspired, and their work is filled with feeling, emotion, and passion. They work to create profitable businesses that empower people and improve their communities.

Though many of us seldom take the time to think about and articulate our reasons for being in business, doing so is essential to creating an exceptional brand and building a great company.

Being aware of the *why* at the core of your business enables you to translate that why into your company's core values, and your core values are, in turn, articulated in your brand.

The word "value" is held to mean the worth or regard in which something is held, that thing's good or usefulness. "Value" can also refer to the judgment of a person or collective of people of what's important, or it can mean their principles or standard of behavior. In short, "value" pertains to whatever is thought to be beneficial or good or important.

Your inner beliefs or core values—those beliefs you hold to be good and important—are the source of the core values of your business. You, as founder of your company, will certainly articulate some of your own personal values as your company's core values. The core values of your business are so important. They don't change in response to market changes; rather, you'd deem it better to change your market in order to remain true to your core values.[1]

---

1. James C. Collins and Jerry I. Porras, "Building Your Company's Vision*,"* *Harvard Business Review* (September–October 1996): 67.

Your core values, that is, your "guiding principles that never change,"[2] in turn, inform your vision for your business. Your vision encompasses the *why* of your business, in addition to what you'd like your business to accomplish, as well as your strategies for actually accomplishing your goals. Your vision for your business also includes how you'd like to be perceived by your employees, your customers, your competition, and your community.

Value **is the result of a way of doing business that ensures your company fulfills the desires of your employees, customers, and community better than any of your competitors and better than anyone has done before, preferably at higher profit margins.**

A thing may have intrinsic value and it may have added value. These two aspects of value articulate the *why* at the heart of your business.

---

2. Ibid.

When we say people are intrinsically motivated, we mean they're working from the inside out. A company understands its *why* in much the same way. Companies with inspired leaders operate from the inside out. You could say these companies are intrinsically motivated.

Companies operating intrinsically are able to create added value for their shareholders, greater perceived value for their customers, and increased value for their brand—or brand value. Brand value is the worth of your brand in the marketplace. Your brand value corresponds to the degree to which your brand is accepted and understood in the market.

Jim Collins, in his bestselling book *Good to Great*, defines a great company as one that has generated a cumulative total stock return of at least three times the general market for the period, from the transition point through year fifteen.

I firmly agree that a rising company valuation at a rate greater than other successful companies sustained over a period of fifteen years is part of what makes a company great. But more than rising valuations, a really great company, large or small, is striving for something bigger than itself.

It could be striving to be the largest company in its field. It could be seeking to make the world a better place by contributing to some important aspect of the environment. It could be desirous of being the very best at something or being a thought leader in its field.

Whatever a great company's reason for being, at its core are inspired, passionate people striving to achieve a big vision they all share and improve the quality of people's lives.

Metrics are an important component of any business. I'm a firm believer that if you don't measure it, you'll never be effective at improving it.

Though there's no metric for love or heart, Heart is the single most important factor in brand value, and brand value is the cornerstone of a great business.

CHAPTER 4
OWN YOUR INTELLIGENCE

Everyone's born with talent, be it in one area or several. *Talent* is an aptitude you may have for a particular activity that you develop over time until you completely master it. Though everyone's born with talent, we may not always recognize ours. In fact, there are some people who, sadly, believe they have no talent.

Talent has long been regarded as some kind of special ability mystically bestowed upon a fortunate few who shine in the heavens like stars. In many instances, talent is associated with a particular discipline, like music or dance, or a branch of the sciences, and people talented in those disciplines are thought to be exceptional, different from other people, only a little lower than the gods.

However, talent may be more of a strength or clarity in a particular sensory mode—for example, the ability to perceive especially clearly through one's inner eye, or to hear particularly sharply with one's inner ear, or to apprehend the unspoken "vibes" of another through one's soul—which enables one to excel in his or her discipline of choice.

Perhaps the true areas of talent are these inner qualities that allow us to approach artistic or scientific disciplines in amazingly impressive manners.

I like Howard Gardner's theory of multiple intelligences, which substitutes the word "intelligence" for "talent"—and by doing so demystifies and democratizes the notion of *talent*.

Gardner suggests that intelligence can be broken out into three categories. He says intelligence is 1) the ability to gather new knowledge, which makes it possible to create solutions to problems, 2) the possession of skills that make it possible to solve problems, and 3) the ability to offer effective products and services that are of value in a culture.

He suggests that intelligence, rather than being just one ability, can be differentiated into nine "modalities." Everyone is strong in one or another of the modalities, or several of them simultaneously.

People who are strong in a **musical** modality have a high sensitivity to musical sounds, rhythms, and tones. Such people are able to sing, play musical instruments, and compose music. Those whose strength lies in a **visual** modality can visualize with the mind's eye and are able to solve spatial or navigational problems.

Verbal individuals are very good with words and language. Such people are good at reading, writing, and memorizing words, and they're excellent storytellers; while **logical** people are very good at logic, reasoning, numbers, and critical thinking. **Kinesthetic** people can handle objects skillfully, have good timing, and learn by movement. Such people are great athletes, dancers, and actors and are also outstanding at construction.

Interpersonal people are skillful at interacting with other people, are sensitive to others' feelings, and like to cooperate; and **intrapersonal** people are introspective, with a deep understanding of themselves and an awareness of their strengths, weaknesses, and what makes them unique.

Naturalistic people are very good at nurturing. They enjoy seeking and communicating information about humanity and their natural surroundings. People who are strong in the **existential** modality have spiritual intelligence.

Though the theory of multiple intelligences categorizes abilities in this manner, there's often significant overlap, with people having distinct strengths in several of these areas simultaneously.

It's important to know where your intelligence lies, and it's important to own your intelligence, because this is what empowers you to perform extraordinary and heart-centered actions.

When you own your intelligence, you operate from your place of genius, and your work is inspired, for it's fueled by your creative energy.

This is the source of authenticity in your conversation and your actions, to which others respond intuitively and positively, and by which your actions are thought to be intrinsically motivated. So know where you're intelligent.

Own your intelligence!

CHAPTER 5
THE COMING OF AGE OF THE BRAND

Branding, traditionally, was a mark. It was your logo, something that was at the top of your letterhead, on your business card, and on the side of your truck. For products, brand identity was the logo you put on it, a trademark.

I remember back in the 1960s, listening to my grandmother, my aunt, and my mom talk about how my teenaged cousin preferred certain brands, or marks, to others. They thought it odd.

My cousin's generation had more choices than her mom's and certainly more than our grandmother's. I think that as large retail companies offered buyers more choices they also created the means by which buyers could make those choices more quickly and in a more finely tuned manner. This is one of the motivators for the creation of the brand. And so if you wanted jeans, you'd look at what your favorite designer was offering first and then move on from there. I don't think anyone was identifying with brands when there were just a couple of choices.

Branding helped people identify with companies and their products. My dad was a Chevy guy who liked GM and had friends who favored Ford. He associated the values of durability, strength, and reliability with Chevy, and he liked the vehicles' styles as well. Those characteristics were what he identified with himself, and he was proud if people thought the same of him.

Heart: Building A Great Brand in the Digital Age

My father, born at the beginning of the Great Depression, was very careful with his money. He thought GM was a better company, producing a superior product. During the seventies, when Japan was exporting more cars to the United States, my father also liked that GM was an American company. So even way back, people were identifying with brands that offered the things they loved. My dad was a real car guy through and through, but never did care about clothes. Still doesn't to this day.

In the twentieth century, your brand was your logo. In the twenty-first century, your brand is your voice, your vision, your values, your meaning, and your purpose--not so much what you're selling, but how people identify with what you believe.

Your company's brand emerges from the discovery of and focus upon the values that are important to you. Your brand is the visible and tangible answer to the question: "*Why* am I doing this?" Your brand is the experience others have of your answer to this question.

Your brand wields tremendous power when people identify with it.

CHAPTER 6
EVOLUTION OF THE BRAND IN THE DIGITAL AGE

The exigencies of the evolving digital age have brought into being a number of new ideas. Some of the most exciting of these ideas owe much to the praxis of twenty-first century entrepreneurs turned on by the possibilities opened up by new technologies, yet facing the challenges of building profitable businesses in the face of the uncertainties created by those technologies.

Leaders of established companies charged with the mandate to rethink old paradigms of leadership, and marketers navigating uncharted paths opened up by a multiplicity of social platforms are also contributing new ideas to this era's collective pool of knowledge. So are ordinary people every day.

By digital economy, I refer to a business and social environment with an emerging digital infrastructure, one in which analog and physical content is being translated into digital code and in which networks such as the Internet, intranets, and mobile devices facilitate the sharing of digital information. Within this environment, business as usual is digital business, digital commerce, and social business.

This doesn't mean that the old analog and brick-and-mortar entities are no longer relevant. Rather, they exist in close and sometimes uncomfortable proximity to their digital counterparts and rivals.

Within this exciting and often-unnerving business environment, the old maxims of the industrial economy that depersonalized the workplace with impunity in the name of profit have had to give way to more people-centered perspectives (also in the name of profit). This is because of the unprecedented success of technology in empowering people to use the influence of their connections to demand greater accountability from businesses. The kid next door with her nose glued to her phone 24/7 literally has millions of brands at her fingertips—in contrast to my cousin back in the 1960s—and unlimited power to choose. Or not.

In this environment, a twenty-first-century tech equivalent of the Wild West, doing business with heart becomes more than a personal choice; it has become imperative. Because business has become personal. And consumers themselves have made it so.

Consumers now have the means by which they can access in-depth knowledge about your brand before they purchase it. Product reviews and ratings allow first-hand user experience of every brand to be published across a spectrum of platforms. Anyone with a phone can research your brand's niche, find your brand, discover what others have said about their experiences of your brand, and make up their minds on the spot whether to give your brand a try.

The information consumers seek and find allows them to distinguish between what a brand says about itself and what it actually is. The ease and speed with which people can share information about your brand potentially alters a consumer's relationship with it, since it's a relatively easy thing for anyone to try another brand through the influence of unlimited and simultaneous reach.

In our digital economy, people can demand a superior brand experience and, because of the power of social sharing, hold a reasonable expectation that their demands will be met.

The digital economy has brought to prominence several features, some of which are new and others of which are acquiring increasing acceptance and significance. All of them have forced us to continually evolve our thinking about our brands.

Perhaps the most glaring feature is the digitalization of everything. People live "Internet lives" and do virtually everything online. Personal life events, including childbirths and funerals, are streamed online beside any and every kind of public performance. In fact, global audiences can consume private events, and one can consume global events in private.

Once-analog entertainment like television and radio have also become digitized and both are widely available on the Internet. This has forced large media networks to redesign their business models.

Print content is being digitalized as well. The book, the newspaper, and the magazine are no longer the only means by which the word can be consumed; people enjoy the work of their favorite authors on e-readers and on their phones as well as on their laptops and other electronic devices. This has afforded greater importance and prominence to e-publishing and self-publishing (or independent publishing) processes, facilitated the emergence of hybrid publishing goliaths like Amazon.com, and forced traditional publishing houses to completely re-envision their place and status as gatekeepers of knowledge.

Entire libraries are now digitally accessible from computers and mobile devices, and schools and universities have integrated technology into the delivery of education to give learners expanded, tech-driven access to knowledge. This has significantly altered the way people receive and process information, as well as the speed with which they process it. It has permanently altered the way people read and write.

Such innovations have given rise to a challenge to traditional notions of copyright and ownership of intellectual and artistic property as a result of massive sharing capabilities, along with a correlating increase in governmental regulation of digitally contexted activities and the increase of state surveillance.

Consumerism is more rabid than ever yet is articulated within smooth, humanist rhetoric. A significant feature of twenty-first century consumerism is the rise of e-commerce, which allows consumers to conduct monetary transactions instantly and in real time, from any location, 24/7. You can sell virtually anything to an unlimited number of customers who aren't constrained by what you sell in your store.

In fact, there's no need for anyone to travel to your store. For many people, purchasing a product can be done from their laptops in their living rooms or from their phones while they stroll through a park, using online sites designed for instant, hassle-free, and timesaving shopping.

The ubiquitous nature of e-commerce is paralleled by an explosion in the number of social sharing platforms, which have become a staple in people's lives and facilitate commerce as easily as they do intimate, personal interaction. This is why inbound marketing has become so indispensable to businesses. Marketers, realizing how much time people devote to social sharing, have taken their business where the people are, and this has virtually eliminated the old public space–private space dichotomy that defined previous economic paradigms.

Along with the social platforms are many adjunct platforms created for the sole purpose of helping people simultaneously manipulate multiple sharing sites at maximum efficiency.

These and other futuristic innovations are juxtaposed with ancient intangibles like "spirit." Also coming into prominence is interest in in-the-moment or mindful living enriched by non-Western ideas that seem to assuage Western tech-induced angst.

Mindfulness as part of classroom education is also happening, so is increased interest in neuroscience, which serves as a demystifier of previously sacrosanct religious and artistic ideas. Mindfulness education is also one of the many innovations in the delivery of education as a response to the diverse ways in which technology has altered the way people process information.

All this is taking place within the phenomenon of multicultural societies, by no means new a phenomenon, but one becoming more prominent due to the vast scope of global migration. As our world becomes larger, yet smaller, due to people's increasing boldness in transgressing national boundaries (to the chagrin of governmental and law-enforcement agencies), unfamiliar designs for social living expressed in language, art, cuisine, entertainment, family structures, etc., are transforming hitherto familiar cityscapes and communities all over the globe.

This has encouraged intellectual, artistic, and activist discussion of ethnicity, nationality, and racial identity to become more prominent and structured, though no easier to navigate. The same goes for gender. The old divisions of labor are crumbling as gender lines and roles become blurred in the face of a clear shift from industrial economies.

Prominent features of a world like this include a focus on environmental issues, an emphasis on "circular" (recycling) economies, an interest in plant-based nutrition and healing, a passion for the rights of animals, and a support of small communities, small farms, and local businesses.

Social environments are pausing to consider the rights of the powerless and the environment with an activist sense of urgency, and the individual is liberating him- or herself from the dominance of monopolistic business, governmental, corporate, and ecclesiastical interests.

As I contemplate how our world is changing every day, I'm struck by the irony that, despite the ability of anyone to communicate with anyone else at any time, there seems to be an increase in people's senses of alienation and aloneness. And I wonder: Did the technology give rise to the alienation, or did a rising alienation create a demand for the technology?

In a world of increasing mass consumption, there seems to be a more prominent emphasis on more individual, *unique*, and even *interior* experiences shaped by a pervasive angst peculiar to this age.

Thus, a company's brand is of primary importance, and your ability to tell a meaningful story--not only about your business, but about you--has become critical to your success. Your story—the why of your business—is integral to your brand. It's central to the delivery of your product, and it's central to your creating a persona of integrity on the social media platforms, which themselves have become central to creating and maintaining trust.

If the folks I know trust and like you, then I will trust and like you, too. A product is discovered as much by likes, friends, and interests as by direct sales driven by features and price.

The principles of heart—integrity, truth, honesty, keeping your word, working according to the highest interpersonal and business principles—are of vital importance to exponentially increasing your brand's value in the marketplace.

Through your brand, you create value in an economy that's forced to continually create new value in ways that didn't previously exist in order to set you apart from your competitors. The key is in the transparency, accountability, and generosity of your brand.

Your brand has two aspects. One is experiential and the other is metaphoric. The experiential aspect of your brand flows from your company's core values and is the *experience* your employees and customers have of your company's reason for being. The metaphoric aspect of your brand includes any number of actions, activities, sounds, ideas, symbolism, and imagery that reinforce and articulate the values at the heart of your company. Both aspects of your brand arise from your beliefs and your values.

Your brand is built around what you do and why. How successful your company becomes begins with your core values and beliefs, which radiate through all levels of management, right down to your front line, and define your company's culture.

People buy *why* you're in business first, and then they buy what you sell. This is because the rational, decision-making neocortex center of the brain is strongly—and unconsciously—influenced by the limbic brain, which is the seat of our gut decisions, our feelings, and our impulses toward truth. We are, so to speak, hardwired to make intuitive, gut decisions.[3]

Before we make decision in our heads, we have already made them in our hearts. As a result, people don't buy what you sell; rather they buy based on an indescribable feeling they have. We call it a gut decision, and it's based on what they *feel* about what you're doing. More specifically, it's about the *why*. The cause.

Your customers are motivated by what you believe. If you talk about what you believe, you'll attract the people who believe in your cause, who believe what you believe. These people will become your clients, your employees, your fans, and your evangelists. This heartfelt connection is the communication to your prospective customers of what you believe.

---

3. Simon Sineck, *Start with Why*, London: Penguin Books, 2009.

When you can inspire your customers, employees, and community through the articulation of the core beliefs within your brand, your business will have the potential not only to outperform its competitors, but also to perform better than any business in its field has ever done.

The core values at the heart of your business—the values you validate within your business—will empower you to create a unique vision for your business and a unique brand.

CHAPTER 7
BELIEVE IN WHAT YOU SELL: A HEART-CENTERED SALES PROCESS

You can't fake heart. If you do, people will see it before you even get to the door. Be genuine, be yourself, and honestly be interested in the people you're calling on, not as prospects but as people.

Salespeople who close at seventy percent, fifty percent, or even thirty percent are communicating your brand and articulating your company's reason for being, its cause. They're getting to the *why,* the heart of your company, its higher purpose, and they're doing it by appealing to the emotions of your prospective clients. Such master salespeople connect with your clients, not at the level of the mind, but at the level of the heart. A heartfelt connection between you and your client is essential to creating a satisfying, lifelong relationship.

Seeking that heartfelt connection with clients is one of the core values of my own business, the one I regard as a key ingredient in the success formula of my company as well as the companies I've worked with and helped reach the top of their markets.

A heartfelt connection is successful because this approach is entirely in sync with the natural decision-making process of the brain. It works because people resonate with your passion. The combination of passion and expertise is what gets you 70 percent close rates.

Sales and marketing is the communication of the essence of your brand. It's the messaging of your vision to your target demographic as well as to potential and current employees, and as such, is a means of creating and exponentially increasing your brand's value.

I follow a sales process comprising nine steps, which, if followed, will enable any salesperson to realize significant success in sharing his or her brand with others.

1. **Warm-Up/Entry**

    Dale Carnegie, in his book *How to Win Friends and Influence People*, says that in order to be interesting to people, one must be interested in those people. I think this is the one thing salespeople can't learn. If you don't like people, if you're only interested in yourself, there's no way you can be successful at sales.

    Your entry into a sales discussion is very much the same as what happens when you meet new people. You're likely going to spend the next hour with them. It'd be a shame not to get to know who they are as people. It's likely you'll have some points of connection that will help you get closer to them, allow you to like them more, and enable them to get to know you as well.

2. **Needs Assessment and Analysis/Customer Qualification (Are they a good fit for your company?)**

    If you're on a sales call, there's a reason you're there. In this step you find out why. Why did that person call you or accept your request to visit him or her?

There are very few people who will allow a salesperson to sit with them without a reason. Find out what it is. This step starts the process of uncovering whether your company is a good match for the situation, needs, or desires of the prospect and is necessary for all types of businesses.

This part of the process is a reiteration of the lead qualification process you should have done on the phone before going to the sales call. You go over your understanding of why he or she called you or accepted your request for a visit. Ask lots of questions during this step. This is likely the most important information you'll receive. Get all the details you can of the situation. Take notes, draw pictures, or photograph the area.

If you honestly feel you can help, talk about things your company has done in the past and how you or your production people handled situations, needs, or desires that were similar to what this potential client is describing.

From the moment you called or met this person, you've been establishing your credibility and building trust. In this step, you seek to establish trust in the competency of your company. Show what your company does and how it relates to his or her situation. Judge his or her response for realistic expectations about what can be done. Remember: You always want to set up your company to wow the socks off every new customer. Ask lots of questions.

During this phase, you should ask for the budget, if appropriate, or give indications of what you think a project like this will cost. It's important during this step to introduce the prospect to the realities of the expense involved.

3. **Company Story**

At this point, you talk about the *why*—your company's brand—and its meaning for you. Talk about the company's owners, its employees, and the community it serves.

Talk about how the company got started, why it's doing things the way it does, how the company is helping people. Talk about the service people. Are they certified? What goes into their training? Talk about the production process. How was it developed? Why does it make sense to do it the way it's done? Give examples of projects the company has done, how these projects are pertinent to the current situation. Depending on what you're selling, you may do this while showing a portfolio of your work.

4. Service or Product Demonstration

For a service, this is a walk through the area needing the service or a demonstration of how your service or product works. Get familiar with the area and get the prospect familiar with your product or service. Ask about his or her desires, and point out positives and opportunities for enhancement. Ask more questions that will help you develop a solution that meets the prospect's needs or desires. During this step, show your expertise. For a product, give a product demonstration or a test drive. Ask about the budget if you haven't done it yet.

If you've ascertained that he or she is a good fit for your company, offer a solution, though if you're selling a product, you may skip this step. If it's a one-visit solution-development scenario, take measurements. Do your calculations. Create the specifications in order to identify and develop a proposal. Then prepare a proposal. If you're unable to prepare a proposal on site at that time, set an expectation for any necessary further onsite proposal preparation, revisits, or research. Let the prospect know what will happen and what to expect and when.

5. Customer Fulfillment Process Explanation.

Your customer fulfillment process is how you produce what it is you're selling. At this point, talk about what makes your fulfillment processes unique, the special care your company takes that others don't. How you take the time to do the things that will never be seen, but if not done, will affect the performance of the product or service. How the care and attention to every detail adds value for the customer.

Talk about how these systems and procedures relate to the brand, to the company's reason for being and why you do it the way you do. Let your heart and passion shine through your descriptions and explanations.

6. Solution Presentation with References to Needs Assessment

Fully explain the process you went through to arrive at your proposed solution.

7. Present Your Price and the Terms upon Which You'd Like to Be Paid

Create a formula for arriving at your price. In addition, keep in mind this simple value equation: quality + price = extraordinary results that exceed expectations.

8. Ask for the Business

Answer any questions and provide follow-up information if something comes up that you can't answer on the spot. Get signatures and a check.

9.   **Wrap-Up**

Ask if there are any further questions. Thank him or her for the business. Give your contact information. Explain what will happen from there and offer to check back in with him or her. Begin the order fulfillment process.

Though my nine-step sales process is a proven formula for success in sales, when your heart is in your sales approach you don't need to follow a script. Selling with heart means you're courteous and respectful and that you treat others as you'd want to be treated and in a way that reflects well upon you and your company. You'll find the right words for each moment, for selling with heart is selling with honesty and with integrity.

CHAPTER 8
THE MEDITATION GARDEN

The American Cathedral in Paris is located in the eighth arrondissement, between the river and Champs-Élysées. It's a beautiful part of the city with chestnut trees lining both sides of Avenue George V.

Within this luxurious setting stands the church, a huge stone building constructed in the late 1800s, with marble floors and stained glass windows so high up off the ground you don't notice them as you walk by. What you see from the street is stone and wrought iron. But once inside, the church is magnificent.

If you walk out the back of the church and go to the offices, or if you arrive at the church reception area and go to the offices directly, you use a cloistered walkway where a meditation garden sits just to your left. Anyone visiting the church offices, using the rehearsal space for the choir, or going to the kitchen would walk by it.

I've always noticed plants, gardens, and landscapes. When I was a kid, my father would always ask me what I thought about the plants and gardens we saw as we drove around. And so, naturally, I noticed the garden the first time I walked by it, that it didn't complement the gorgeous architecture of the church. It wasn't particularly weedy or unattended; it just didn't sing. There was nothing in it to draw one's attention to it.

The garden separated the church from the apartment of the dean of the church, a gregarious person as interested in his parishioners as they were in him. He walked through the space at least four times a day, I'm sure.

One day, as we were in conversation, I mentioned to Dean Leo that I had a degree in horticulture, and he asked me what I thought of the garden. Sensing an opportunity, I told him I didn't think it popped, and soon enough we were arranging a trip to Rungis, the wholesale market for lots of different goods sold in and around Paris, including plants and flowers. It's an amazing place, huge and well organized.

Before going out to buy the plants, I took an inventory of what was planted in the garden and its current state of health. After that, I made some determinations about what would stay and what would go, developed a plant list, and went off to Rungis.

At this point, I spoke "Franglais," which is like "Spanglish"--a broken French with English words interspersed. The French seem to love and hate our language and truly love theirs. I imagine my Franglais drove them batty. I'd been living in France only six months or less, and I could say *bonjour, au revoir*, and *ooh, la, la*.

With the help of Dean Leo's wife, Patsy, whose French was much better than mine, I was able to purchase everything I'd specified, or if not, a decent substitute. Then it was back to get started on the job of planting.

I'd learned my way around a shovel from years of laboring with my dad in his company. I laid out all the new material and then went about taking out the plants I wanted to remove and doing the necessary transplanting.

As you can imagine, there was a lot of questioning of my knowledge by the older ladies who helped out around the church, who wanted to know who'd given me authority to pull out plants. Their comments were all in French, and I didn't really understand what they were saying, which was probably for the better. But I certainly could understand the tone of their voices and the meaning behind their wagging fingers.

Thankfully, Paris is in a climate zone not too different from Connecticut, a bit more temperate, but very similar, and the plant choices I made worked out great. By the time I was done with it, the garden was colorful and healthy looking, and everyone loved the results of my work.

A church experience is, of course, religious, but the experience is always influenced by its place. This space for worship outside the church was incredible. Inside the church there was an awesome Dupré organ, one of the largest in Paris.

The sanctuary was made of stone and marble, and the acoustics were amazing. It was a great place to sing and worship. The organ's beautiful tone and power reverberating through the church and out into the garden was emotional and moving.

The garden was a beautiful contrast to the huge cut-stone walls surrounding it. The quietness of the garden with the small fountain at its center, in the center of Paris, was luxurious in a totally different way from the majesty of the large old chestnut trees outside along the street. Beauty, spirituality, music, and place. My heart was singing. I was singing. I was doing two of the things I'm best at, and it made people happy. It made me happy.

I've always followed my heart, that part inside that helps me make decisions that I can't put into words. Have I been lucky because I've been able to do the things I'm passionate about? Singing, planting, designing, selling, running businesses, and consulting. I've done them, and I love doing them.

One of the most powerful urges we have as humans is to express ourselves. I think we're happiest when we're expressing what's in our hearts. And heartfelt expression can come through anything, from digging ditches to singing songs, to running businesses.

Is it a choice to love what we do and express ourselves in doing it? Yes, I think it is. I think our hearts can be employed in our actions in any type of honest work we do. There are people who say and think they can't find their lives' passions. I don't think it's that they haven't found the things that make their hearts sing; it's that they haven't found how to engage their hearts in what they're doing.

It's the same in business. The secret is in finding how to engage your heart into your business. If you do, you'll also discover how to employ your heart in the branding of your business. From there, heartfelt marketing and management will follow naturally. The impact of that will resound through all aspects of your business, throughout the community, and beyond.

CHAPTER 9
THE (HE)ART OF BRANDING

Business is an art. Yes, there are metrics and systems as well. Business is structured and at times damn confining, but so is art. Art is defined through its limitations. Every art form has structure. Painters are confined to their media of paint, canvas, or walls. Singers: the composition, composers, the voice. Writers: their imagination and blank paper, or nowadays, blank computer screens.

Every artist is concerned with the structural limitations of his or her art form and his or her ability to communicate within that form. There are many artists, though, who deliberately transgress those limitations, thus creating new genres of art. Jazz music emerged from the transgression of certain structural limitations found in Western music. Cubism and the stream-of-consciousness style emerged from similar transgressions in painting and prose fiction respectively.

We judge art according to the artist's ability to make us feel what he or she feels passionately about. Great art makes us feel something outside of our own existence. Great artists *communicate.*

Like great art, every business can serve a higher purpose, have meaning, and contribute to the community a sum greater than its parts. There are no exceptions. Stephen Schwartz, in his musical adaptation of Studs Turkel's *Working,* illustrates how being a fine waitress can be considered an art if one's heart is in it. And if you're communicating your love for the work you do, people will respond.

That's the essence of branding—communicating from your heart through your business. Your business will be a reflection of what's in your heart. There's no commodification of that. Your unique selling proposition is obvious. Competition?
There will be others competing with you. If you're a waitress, sure, other waitresses will compete. If you're in a gardening business, yes, other gardening businesses will be your competition. But what's in your heart will appeal to your target market like none of the other businesses.

Furthermore, if your heart is in your brand, then your brand will attract employees that resonate with the message, meaning, and intent of your brand.

When people find meaning in their work, it shows. It shows in the quality of their work and in the level of satisfaction they have in their work. They want to learn all they can to increase their skills, and their happiness about what they do increases. Your customers, in turn, are happy and feel the joy your customer service people have in executing your customer service work.

The salespeople attracted to the core values in your heart and in your brand will naturally be passionate about what they do and about what your company does. Passionate sales people, following a carefully designed sales process, will consistently close over 50 percent of the calls they go out on.

Systems and heart. You see the pattern here? Its pretty clear how heart can make your business meaningful and profitable and empower it to grow.

Experiential Branding: Give your customers a memorable and satisfying brand experience by reaching beyond the features and benefits of your product or service to your inner beliefs about why you do your work.

Jason was the owner of an irrigation company that upgraded irrigation systems with smart controllers. He designed upgraded irrigation systems that use 40 percent less water and improve the health of the landscapes they irrigate.

Up to that point, Jason's marketing and branding focused on the features and benefits of his upgraded systems, which accomplished astonishing results. But during our conversations, it became apparent that what was really getting the results was his vigilant monitoring programs and the horticultural expertise he and his employees brought to their work. His passion and skill were what really made the difference.

As I probed deeper into his process, it became clear that his method of analyzing and understanding the conditions of an irrigation system required a very thorough knowledge of agronomy, horticulture, specific site conditions, some plumbing, hydraulics, computer programming, and design. Jason would analyze these factors affecting each system before making his recommendations and a proposal for upgrades. As a result of his analysis he would actually redesign the system.

His upgraded irrigation systems were specified to accommodate all the existing site conditions plus the horticultural requirements of the plants in the garden. He would also specify system upgrades that would have the capacity to monitor the system in its entirety and communicate data to the designated system manager.

When I looked over all he was doing in this process, it became clear that Jason was three things: a skilled horticulturist, a savvy computer programming geek, and a talented irrigation designer.

Jason believed that, in his region, irrigation systems weren't designed and installed in a way that would be most beneficial to property owners and managers. He believed that, through programming, physical and electronic monitoring, and minimum upgrades, he could provide systems that would use less water, make gardens healthier and stronger, and be vital for the life of the garden.

He believed it, he was doing it, and he was getting the results. That was his brand.

CHAPTER 10
FAILURE AS A RITE OF PASSAGE

I've learned way more from my mistakes than I have from any successes I might have attained.

When my own business started to decline in the 1990s I had no clear idea why. I had no background in business management. I was a passionate young man who had been trained in art, performance, music, and horticulture. I thought that if I grew the revenue of my business everything would get better.

I think that even then, the year before I closed my business, I suspected that whether or not I could grow sales, the next year would be my last as a business owner. But I couldn't clearly understand why.

I didn't have a clear plan for the future. I had no systemization in my business. I didn't know what my costs for completed jobs were and couldn't project what costs would be on jobs I was pricing for proposals.

I knew what everyone else was charging, and I thought my company's work was as good as any of my competitors—I actually thought my work was better—and I priced accordingly.

I was a good salesperson, and I communicated the value of our work to customers during sales presentations and won most of the work I presented. During the last year of my company's existence, I grew revenue by 30 percent at the end of the year, but I was no further ahead in paying off my debt than I had been in the beginning. I was probably worse off.

I made the decision to make a negotiated settlement with my credit card companies, and I paid all of my other creditors over time. It was a very difficult time for me and everyone associated with my business. It still stings to think about it, even now, fourteen years later.

I had failed.

At the time I was going through it, I got some good advice from my accountant. With his numbers background and his perspective from outside my company, he saw things I hadn't seen at that point. The things he saw are the things I now know I was doing wrong, and what I now, as a business mentor, help people to get right.

My heart was in my business, but I was like most small business owners. I had a lot of passion for what I did and this propelled my sales efforts, but I had no real brand definition other than the force of my personality. It was all about me. There was no real consideration of what my customers wanted. I didn't have any perspective of my place, what I could offer, and how my business impacted or could benefit the community. I had no systems for anything. My business could only grow to the point that I could organize it.

My accountant counseled me on how to get back on top of my business. I didn't take his advice.

Everyone needs a different set of eyes now and then. But it's not just having a different set of eyes. The person looking at your situation needs to be trained in what to look for. I think anyone trained in business management and coaching can be helpful. Mentoring, too, is a process. If your mentor understands the process and you trust him or her, you and your business can benefit greatly.

The difference, though, is when you heed the advice your mentor gives.

CHAPTER 11
LEADERSHIP AND THE PRAXIS OF HEART-CENTERED BRANDING

A great company is a manifestation of its leader's vision and adds value to the lives of its employees, its customers, and its community.

Leaders who lead with heart guide their companies to their better, truer selves. At the center of his leadership style is the leader's heart. Heart-centered leadership isn't formulaic, and it's not scripted. It's spontaneous, authentic, and real. Leading in this manner is truly an act of love—love for your business, your employees, and the community you serve. Perhaps one reason there's so little leadership around may be that we're afraid to even say the word *love*.

I've encountered business leaders who possessed superior skill sets, which included well-developed knowledge bases as well as the practical skills associated with their fields of endeavor. Yet, without heart, without the motivation to place people at the center of everything they do, they were, without exception, unable to run their companies at maximum efficiency.

A leader of a company destined for greatness has a solid knowledge of his or her field of endeavor, understands how to translate this knowledge into efficient business systems, and knows how to diffuse this information with heart throughout every level of the company. By virtue of this praxis of heart, a leader creates a great brand and exceptional brand value in the marketplace.

With regard to organizations, a significant feature of our digital economy is that people have become more important than ever to the success of businesses.

Face it. Your employees have access--to information, career choices, freelance and independent contractor opportunities, and infinite opportunities for education through both traditional educational institutions attuned to emerging career trends and a myriad of online education centers made possible by digital technology. And a lot of this information is available free of cost. Your people value the ability to be creative and innovative in the workplace as they build their careers around what the market needs.

The traditional obedience-driven leadership role is giving way to one that ideally facilitates employees' continuous development of their core intelligences in the service of strategic positioning of companies in this fiercely competitive digital economy.

Gender roles have become less rigid as the old divisions of labor fade into the past. This means that the guy who runs your operations department can opt to become a stay-at-home dad and earn income working on his Mac from his office at home.

To many, their careers no longer consist of lifetimes spent with one company through which they chart long and steady treks up the corporate ladders, but are more series of significant assignments and projects designed to build portfolios of accomplishments through which they can step out on their own any time. Such individuals are aware of their market worth. And they're mobile.

As a leader, one of your critical functions is to connect the perceived value of your industry to your employees' desires as you guide your company through the convoluted and unchartered jungle of the digital economy.

The old-school manager who sees his employees as resources to be managed is an anachronism in today's digital culture. Your employees are as critical to your brand as your customers, and like your customers, they're perfectly capable of switching brands on you any time. It is up to you, as a leader, to cultivate their loyalty.

As you lead your business, it's important to stay connected to your core values and to the brand your company represents.

If you create an environment where people can be themselves, *feel* your brand, and agree with your core values, you'll foster an environment of trust in which your employees feel safe and in which they thrive.

Staying connected to your brand means continually recreating the experiential aspect of your brand within your company—that is, your company's culture—and this continues to support the aspirations of your employees.

Great Place to Work is a research organization that has designed metrics by which to measure and assess the world's most successful companies. Based on research of more than six- thousand organizations in fifty countries, representing over ten million employees, Great Place to Work has defined what's a great workplace. There are two lenses through which to view a great workplace—the employee lens and the management/leadership lens.

From the employee viewpoint, trust is the most important feature of a great workplace, and what counts the most in creating trust is management's credibility. Trust is also created when employees feel they're treated fairly and with respect. Employees deem a workplace to be great when they can take pride in what they do and when there's such a high level of camaraderie they enjoy the people they work with.

From the leadership perspective, a great workplace is one in which employees give of their personal best and work together as a family in order to achieve the organization's objectives.

Great Place to Work has identified nine areas in which leaders cultivate a culture of trust:

- A great workplace achieves organizational goals by
    - inspiring,
    - speaking, and
    - listening.
- In a great workplace, employees give of their personal best by
    - thanking,
    - developing, and
    - caring.

- Within a great workplace, everyone works together by
  - hiring,
  - celebrating, and
  - sharing.

When a company can create a culture in which its employees are inspired and give their best, that company is well on its way to becoming great.

CHAPTER 12
THE SCIENCE OF BRANDING

If business is an art, it's also a science; that is, it's an organized body of knowledge that has rational explanatory power and processes that can be replicated. Entrepreneurs don't commonly refer to this organized, replicable body of knowledge as science; we usually speak of this aspect of business as "systems."

The terms "business systems" and "systemization" refer to standard operating procedures for all the processes of your business, including training, task delegation, and accountability. Every business owner must have a systemization plan that discovers, prioritizes, documents, implements, and manages all the processes of his or her business.

Without carefully designed systems, your business won't achieve all you've envisioned it to. Without efficient business systems, your workflow will be chaotic and you'll be unable to grow your business beyond a dependency on yourself and your key employees. The situation would be such that you feel you've hit a virtual wall.

To scale your business beyond this virtual wall, you must have carefully thought-out and well-functioning systems.

When your employees have systems *through which to work*, they can work more efficiently because they better understand their work. They appreciate how their work fits into the overall objectives of the company, and this encourages and empowers them more easily and quickly to adapt to your company's culture and give of their personal bests.

The first step in developing systems for your business is to name the processes necessary in each of the four parts of your business. It's often hard to know where to start, but *where* isn't important; it's important that you do start. You can start with any part of your business or with any particular position.

If you own or manage a business that isn't documenting processes, procedures, or protocols but you have an employee who's very effective at getting his or her work done and you as the owner or manager really don't know exactly what he or she is doing, start with that employee. Have him or her help you write processes or have that employee write them alone, and you edit.

Or if you're doing all the sales for the company, write the systems you use to get that work done. When you feel you want to step back from sales, you'll have documented sales systems you can use to train new salespeople and hold them accountable.

Michael E. Gerber wrote a great book years ago called *The E-Myth Revisited*. His thesis is that if you systematize your business by working *on* it (creating systems that anyone can follow) instead of *in* it (doing the work), you'll have a great business that doesn't depend on just you and your key people to operate well. He says this is what franchisers do and is part of what makes a business turnkey and successful. This is exactly what we all should be doing as business owners and managers.

Interestingly, back when Gerber wrote his book, there were no personal computers and certainly no cloud computing or storage capabilities. With the advent of cloud computing, it's now possible for systems, protocols, and procedures to be available to all your employees everywhere they're working, and for your systems manual to become a living, breathing document that's vital to all of your employees. Plus, the use of the systems can be monitored by managers and owners from anywhere.

This is how a business, large or small, is successfully managed. Part of the systems you'll create are those concerned with the meaning and purpose of your brand. Great, thoughtful customer care can be systematized. It will occur as a result of your people automatically following your company's systems, procedures, and protocols.

If your core values are considered and integrated into your systems, they become woven into the way your business operates. This is the primary factor that drives brand integrity and allows a business to remain faithful to its core values despite expansion. It's the source of your ability to keep vision, purpose, and meaning engaged in the brand.

Creating functional business systems starts with understanding the tasks necessary to sell the work or product. Business systems comprise the processes that happen when you're fulfilling orders, as well as the support and management duties that must happen behind the scenes for the frontline customer service people and everyone else to have what they need, when they need it. There are also processes that need to happen systematically throughout management and in leadership roles as well. With that in mind, it's beneficial to categorize your business into four different areas:

1. Getting the business
2. Doing the business
3. Running the business
4. Guiding the business

Looking carefully into the four areas of your business is a good way to discover and identify guideposts, or categories of systems and processes, within your business. Dividing the business this way enables you to be more thorough in your investigation into the processes for each category and provides you with a more comprehensive understanding of your business as a whole.

1. Getting the Business—Sales and Marketing

We've talked about the importance of branding and the establishment of your values and vision to the success of your marketing and sales efforts. Systematizing this aspect of your business is discovering and identifying the steps necessary to generate leads and convert prospects into sales.

Certain things have to happen in order to create marketing campaigns, even if it's a matter of calling in an outside marketing person to help. The first step is to identify the people who will resonate with your brand's message and create step-by-step processes that will produce the marketing necessary to get your message to your target audience.

Choosing and understanding your target market is the strategic work in marketing. Your marketing systems must include analytical steps and procedures that enable you to know who you'll be serving and what makes the most sense for your company to achieve the greatest possible return. If that means you call someone to help you with your marketing, you must have a system that says who will make that call and when.

Once you've done the strategic work, then it's all tactical—how you best reach this demographic and how you measure your returns. Measuring success on the tactical side of marketing is about systematically applying metrics to your marketing efforts and mathematically deciding what works best. The metrics for marketing boil down to cost/lead. The systems you create for marketing will help you better understand the results you're getting and choose which marketing programs to repeat and when.

Sales systems handle the leads and converts prospects into customers. A good metric to apply to the sales process is what percentage of the leads from marketing converts to customers. This is commonly referred to as the close rate. With our sales process in conjunction with heartfelt branding, I've been able to close at over 70 percent annually. This means that if I go out on 200 sales calls in a year, I come back with 140 new customers. A high sales close rate can significantly reduce the cost of customer acquisition, which is also a very good metric to apply to sales and marketing departments.

2. Doing the Business—Operations

Getting your product or service out to the customer includes the multitude of processes and procedures necessary to produce or service even the most simple of things, such as mowing a lawn. Your systems here and throughout your business must have the brand and your reason for being firmly intertwined into your operations processes. Your systems must standardize the highest quality possible. Customer satisfaction is an aspect of experiential branding in which the products and services you deliver to your clients go over and beyond what they expected. Your systems must standardize the Wow Factor. When developing these systems, consider the following:

- How do you know if your clients are getting what they expected?
- What do you do to make sure your customer receives an experience over and beyond what he or she expected?
- What are your methods for handling customer complaints?
- What do you do to ensure that the quality of your product or service is consistently high?

To help you get to the processes involved in operations, consider the following:

- What are the methods you use to produce your product or service?
- How do you innovate your product or service?
- How do you make sure your product or service does what you intended it to do or promised your customer it would do?
- How do you know whether or not your company is performing to client's expectations?

What are the methods you use to get your product or service to the client?

- If your business is service based:
    - Do you meet in person or on the phone?
    - How do you prepare for those meetings?
    - What's the agenda for those meetings?

- If your business is product based:
    - Do you use a fulfillment house, such as Amazon?
    - What methods do you use for delivery? Are there follow-up processes to make sure your client received what he or she expected?

Metrics for evaluating operations could include
- percent of upsells (enhancements) on orders, products, or services;
- service contracts, percent of customers renewing contracts after completion;
- number of callbacks because of dissatisfaction with product or service; and
- number of referrals.

Creating and fine-tuning your business systems and prioritizing them according to importance is one of your most critical leadership functions.

Consider which systems, if documented and implemented, would be the most beneficial to your business. Document the procedures by which your systems will be executed. Bring on board those members of your staff who actually work with those systems to assist with documenting the systematization process. Implement your systems and monitor the results. Go through your systems document with your staff and encourage discussion about what needs to be done and how. Talk about applicable metrics to judge expected results.

3. Running the Business—Financial and Administration

Systems for running your business aren't directly related to delivering on your promise to your clients, but they're vital to ensuring that your service is delivered in an excellent and professional manner. The systems in this key function fall into the categories of administrative, financial, and human resource processes.

When we speak of administrative processes, we refer to answering the phone, office organization, filing, and greeting clients. Financial processes refer to accounts receivable and payable, general ledger, payroll, budgeting, purchase ordering, and collections. Human resource processes are recruiting, hiring, employee termination, and performance evaluation and employee assessments.

4. Guiding the Business—Leadership/Management

Many businesses don't focus enough on processes that manage employee or business processes. Management or monitoring of the process is as important as the process itself. If you don't monitor your systems and regularly check to see that they're being adhered to, the people executing the systems are as likely to neglect doing them as you are in checking them. Such systems focus on three distinct types of processes:

- *Management Processes*, which ensure that processes are developed and implemented accurately and efficiently and that expectations are monitored and reported. To systematize your management processes, you must consider

- what management systems you use or need, such as sales meetings and manager meetings, and
- what guidelines you have to ensure your meetings are effective and efficient.

- *Board of Director Processes,* which address systems for ensuring compliance with your company's articles of incorporation. If there are other advisory boards that function in your company, consider the processes required for them.
- *Strategy Processes,* which guide your business toward its goal or strategic target and focus on
  - the methods you and your managers use to track progress toward your company's vision and
  - the systems you need to track the progress made on those goals.

An important strategy process in guiding the business is the creation of a strategic target, a well-defined description of the future business you intend to create. Your strategic target answers the question: "How do I want this business to be running when I'm ready to sell it or hand it off to my kids or employees?"

The strategic target is the factual written and publishable description of your business at this end stage and should hang on the wall of your office. The document includes answers to questions such as:

- What will your best clients be like?
- How many will you have?
- How many times a year will they make purchases?
- What would they say if I asked them what's it like to do business with your company?
- How profitable will you be?
- How many employees will you have?
- What will your employees say if you ask them *"What's it like to work there?"*

A study done at the Harvard Business School has found that simply by having this document, you have a 300-percent-better chance of achieving your objectives than if you don't have it—which makes perfect sense, because if you don't really know where you're going, how are you ever going to get there? When you create your strategic target, you can develop an organization chart of that future business.

Unless your business is where you want it to be and you don't intend on having it get any bigger by answering the above questions, you should envision what you'd like your company to become and develop an organization chart based on this vision.

Even though there may not be different people in each position, if you think about it, you'll find that each person in your company is filling multiple roles envisioned in your organization chart.

The organization chart job titles don't represent people; they represent positions. Every company, whether it has one or more employees, needs an org chart to establish and define the functional accountability for each of the four areas of the business.

Each position is expected to perform a function, and the employee filling that position is accountable to that end. Each position on the org chart needs a job description that sets out what the employee is expected to do and how he or she is expected to do what you need done.

"What" and "how" inform the specifics of your processes and create the systems necessary to run your business. The processes are assigned job positions and become the key ingredients for job descriptions.

The chart helps you understand the required human resources you're going to need to accomplish your objectives, and it provides a strategy for growth: who you'll hire next and what you have to do to get that position up to speed quickly as you grow.

How to Build a System

1. Specify the system name.

2. Write the result or the objective.

3. Diagram the steps in the system showing their sequence and how they relate to each other using a simple flow-chart diagram.

4. Write the tasks and expectations of each box on your flow chart.

How to Write a System

The starting point for designing a business system is to define the exact result you want the system to produce. Review your prioritized systems list and choose one specific system. What's the result or goal you wish to accomplish with this system? Think about the end result. What is it that you want to achieve? Write it down. This is what's called the *objective*.

Consider how to achieve that result, and write the broad-stroke steps of the system that could be put in place to achieve it. Use a box and arrow diagram to accomplish this step. Review each of the steps in the flow chart and expand on them with as much detail as you feel is necessary.

Establish and document the expectations you have of someone in your organization following and completing this system. Look at your org chart to determine who will be responsible for making it happen.

Systematization of your business will significantly multiply your chances of growing your business, even beyond your own expectations.

CHAPTER 13
BUILDING YOUR BRAND IN THE TRENCHES

Orange Blossom was a troubled company with many personnel problems. When I first met Peter, the owner, Orange Blossom was in its tenth year of operation and was commanding annual revenue of about 2.2 million dollars. However, the general manager was on the verge of a nervous breakdown, and the whole group of managers was as twitchy as a herd of white tail deer that had just gotten whiff of a coyote.

And they had good reason to be fearful. The company was extremely bloated at the management level, and this created problems throughout all the business processes. Though every single person who worked there was of high caliber--each of them would be a star if well managed and most companies would be pleased to have any of them on their staff--the problem was they weren't being well managed, and the company was suffering because of it. Orange Blossom was neither an easy nor a happy place to work.

The frontline people doing most of the work trusted each other, liked their jobs, and were generally well managed. However, trust was an issue among all of the managers, and there were eight of them. Eight managers meant that the company was extremely top heavy. It was my job to take the helm, right the ship, and lead it on a course of greater prosperity, happiness, and higher sales.

Orange Blossom had been growing consistently since its inception. A year or two before I got there, Peter had purchased a competing company in the market. This helped to grow revenue during some particularly slow economic times. Without this purchase, I don't believe Peter would have seen much growth in revenues for the two years before I got there.

Though Peter had convinced himself that he was positioning himself for growth, the lack of trust and poor management was driving his managers to leave. In addition, he seemed to be distrustful and nervous about the people running his business, me included. As he saw it, he had a lot riding on the growth of the company in terms of opportunity costs.

He felt he took a huge leap of faith to start his business and had a lot of anxiety. He was extremely effective at transmitting his anxiety to the managers.

However, he did recognize there were trust issues and wanted to regain some of the spirit that was in the company when it started but that had faded away over the years.

The main problem was that Peter was absent from the day-to-day activities of the company. He wasn't out of the loop, but he managed another business full time and was checking in at Orange Blossom through weekly meetings with the managers.

Trust issues are extremely hard to overcome, and this was where I needed to start, for the pain the managers were feeling sounded discordant notes throughout the company's operations.

I had to establish credibility and trust among the owners and the staff of managers, working both sides at the same time. It was especially difficult. In addition, I had to come up with a plan to improve the company's operations. It would be wonderful if everyone in the company would just accept the changes I wanted to make and we could move forward to initiate the plan directly. But that's never the case.

Experiential Branding: Let your employees experience fulfillment on the job by investing personal capital—spending the time—in the creation of a culture of trust.

In order to have people trust you, you must trust them first. You need to be honest and authentic. People can smell a phony from miles away.

I used up an awful lot of energy trying to get these guys to loosen up and find the fun in what they were doing and enjoy each other. Peter was trying very hard to do the same. As time went on, he became more involved, and ultimately it was the time that he spent in his company that allowed him to relax more with his employees and allowed them to have a better understanding of who he was as a person.

Peter's methods to gain trust and to get people to enjoy each other was to have social events. He would take the management staff out regularly and really try to win them over. I don't think it was anything he did in particular, but the time he put in worked in his favor, as he's naturally a man of integrity and a very likable guy. He'd just made some management errors and needed time to recover the lost trust.

My way to gain their trust was to spend time with them as well and really make an effort to find the fun in what we were doing. It happened at different rates with everyone. But first, the damage to the company from the prior two years had to work itself through.

Another important component of trust is credibility. Well-designed systems, carefully worked-out protocols and well-articulated procedures establish credibility and are, thus, essential to your business. They're the channels through which your core values are experienced by your employees and your customers.

If your systems are strong and carefully thought out, following the systems and exuding the passion is 99.9 percent of what it takes to gain trust.

And so I developed an action plan designed to strengthen critical areas of the business. The plan would enable us to establish a clear chain of command with clear lines of communication throughout all the tiers of the company, through the development of the company's existing org chart.

My plan was further designed to:
- streamline the maintenance portion of the business and develop two account management positions that would ultimately be accountable for all of the maintenance work;
- raise the level of training at all levels of the company;
- shore up undeveloped portions of the business, such as installation, design build, and design sales;
- create leaner, more efficient systems for pricing, tracking production rates, and recovering overhead expenses; and
- most importantly, *get the team to trust me and follow my lead.*

Experiential Branding: When you create business systems that facilitate and enhance workflow and execute them in a heart-centered manner, your employees will derive satisfaction from their work.

Mountain View was a small family-owned company nestled within in a prosperous commercial zone. They did mostly landscape maintenance and irrigation, along with enhancement work for existing customers and some construction.

I quickly discovered that the company served some of the richest people in the world. Property values were extremely high there, and the beautiful houses were complemented by elegant, tasteful gardens. The owners and managers of Mountain View understood the value of beautifully designed and well-maintained gardens and wanted the best for their properties.

The company, which had been in business for twelve years, had a great deal of competition, for landscaping was important to the community. One company, the largest in the community, with a thirty-year history in the area, dominated the market and garnered most of the business. We were trailing far behind our other competitors. Our annual revenues were around five hundred thousand dollars.

I analyzed the four major components of the business: management, sales, finance, and operations. It soon became clear why it wasn't doing as well as it could. It didn't have a systemization plan.

Important activities like sales and marketing were loosely organized. There was no sales system and no clear marketing plan or intent, though customer service was passable and sales inquires were attended to. Pricing formulas were clunky, job costing was inconsistent, but there was accounting for hours spent by laborers and management with regard to work billable and work performed. Operations was a virtual free-for-all. There were too many people on the maintenance crews. There was no consistency among crews and very little communication between the production staff and management.

Throughout the company there was no employee-skill development or training program. There wasn't any clear chain of command, and job descriptions were vague assumptions of who did what. Nothing was written down; therefore, there was no way to make regular evaluations or clear methods to show employees' paths to position improvement or career development.

Heart-centered leadership will recognize the natural leaders in the team and draw upon their skills to develop significant parts of the business as well as the company's brand.

I was thrilled to discover that there were a number of natural leaders on Mountain View's staff. There was Leroy, who had an eye for detail. I moved him into a crew leader role after some personnel changes were made and eventually pulled him from maintenance and put him in charge of the new landscape construction crew, and eventually the department.

Kendrick, a tough, quiet, honest person, expected people to do the right thing and demanded it from everyone he worked with. He had the necessary discipline to stick to a system in order to accurately determine its effectiveness and was an excellent maintenance crew leader.

Samuel, a ladies man who loved to have fun, had an academic background in pesticide application in addition to such a well-developed knowledge of plants that we created a lawn and plant health-care program around his abilities.

Another one of the leaders on staff was Javier, the company's mechanic, a very intelligent, thoughtful person who had influence with everyone in the company, immediately understood what I was doing, and was extremely helpful in getting the changes implemented. I moved him into a leadership role as well.

Experiential Branding: Heart-centered leadership must integrate core values and efficient business systems to create a company culture that is both comfortable and productive.

The next few weeks were busy at Mountain View. Once I'd made my analysis, I formulated a plan that included system development in all areas of the business. My plan was to implement the program on multiple fronts simultaneously.

Our goal at first was to keep our jobs and keep making the customers happy. But I saw the company's potential for greatness. As I communicated my vision for the company to my staff, our goal became larger; we wanted to be the best at what we did, to develop an extraordinary business. I saw where the problems lay, and as we talked about solutions, our goal morphed into our vision, which was to become the regional leader in landscape maintenance and installations. Our vision was fueled by our core values, which included respect for ourselves, our customers, and our work.

We met every morning at 6:30, and while the crews were getting the trucks and trailers ready for the days work, I--a cup of steaming Jamaica Blue Mountain coffee in hand--would meet with the landscape maintenance manager and each crew leader as needed.

I was always careful to respect the chain of command, and I followed the lines of communication as drawn out in the org chart. But I wanted to maintain an emotional tie with everyone who worked there, and showing up early in the morning helped.

We needed to pull together around something. I gave direction through conversations, stimulating thinking around how we were going to work together to improve the company, keep our jobs, and become great. We developed our core values together.

The core values of your business need to be articulated clearly throughout your company. Everyone, from your managers to your supervisors to your salespeople, right through to all of the frontline service employees should know what they are.

If your vision is clear and communicated throughout your company, the effects of your message will be constant and consistent. Your systems will be executed with your values in view, and when a judgment call has to be made, you'll have the confidence your employees are making decisions based on your shared values and with the ultimate vision of the company in mind. Instances of this happen every day, every time a decision has to be made out in the field.

For example, if one of your core values is respect—treating other people the way you'd like to be treated—then when a decision has to be made out in the field, say, about whether to put a fallen branch in the truck or chuck it over the fence into the neighbor's yard, there's no question about what the final decision will be.

Your company's vision is likely a demonstration of your core values, an articulation of your own beliefs. Much the same way customers buy what you believe, your employees want to feel part of something that's meaningful and has intrinsic value.

I questioned my staff closely about how they did what they did and why. Answers weren't always directly forthcoming, but people walked away with those questions in mind and went about doing what I had asked about. Through my line of questioning they began to understand the logic of what I was doing and where I was headed with my questions. Answers to my questions started to come in from the field, but even before I got all the answers, I began to develop systems with the crew leaders.

Experiential Branding: A leader is willing to get into the trenches with his employees and work with them to develop and fine-tune efficient business systems.

I talked about increasing efficiencies, creating processes or systems for each of the production-related activities in which we engaged, and creating systems for how to utilize three people on a crew instead of four. These systems detailed exactly what was expected of each person on the crew from the moment they arrived at the property to the moment they got back in the truck to go to the next property.

We worked on these systems together. Leroy had grown up on a farm and could handle any tool ever made for farming, I bet, and certainly every tool we were using to get our work done for landscape maintenance and construction. He was a key employee whose knowledge was critical to the development of our landscaping processes.

I asked my staff a lot of questions about what they were currently doing and why. Taking their suggestions into consideration and incorporating them where we could, we created processes around the tasks they were each doing in their jobs and in the jobs of the people they supervised or came into contact with while executing the required work.

I asked for suggestions about how they thought they could improve, become quicker and more efficient. We rerouted for efficiency but tried to keep the crew leaders on the same properties they'd been working on and began to look carefully at everything.

We established the routes and the routine. By repeating them and being open to refinement, we were able to look at what we were doing right and what we needed to look at further. The repetition helped everyone get better at what we were doing, and we tweaked the process if we weren't seeing improvements.

The systems helped to increase efficiency and easily accommodated the one-less person on each crew. This improved the quality of our work, thereby raising our value to our customers. We kept our prices the same on our existing accounts and raised our profit. We talked a lot about value, our value to our customers.

We talked about attention to detail and doing the right thing every time we could. We talked about respecting each other, the customers, and our work. We studied the science of what we were doing, not at a deep research level, but from a pragmatic level of execution, and within the context of what made sense to do or not to do, when, where, and how. I learned a lot from these guys. I brought horticultural experience and study to the table; they brought lifetimes of growing up around and working with plants types and varieties that were totally new to me.

Our systems made us quick and profitable, increased our attention to detail, and improved the quality of our work. The science of horticulture applied to landscape maintenance made us knowledgeable and efficient. The guys liked the direction we were heading and felt part of the process I was initiating for the improvements.

We established systems for bidding work, which allowed us to accurately take information from bid documents and calculate costs. Understanding how long it took to do all the tasks required to accomplish the job as specified allowed us to predict labor and calculate the required amount of profit.

Our job costing and tracking processes allowed us to see how well we fared according to predictions and enabled us to improve our estimates. Being able to predict the costs with precision while fine-tuning our systems enabled us to win work, and this created a positive feedback loop that enabled us to create an upward spiral of success.

As our systems got better, so did our knowledge of production rates. Tighter bids closer to actual costs allowed me to confidently know more precisely what my walk-away price was and to choose when I wanted to be more competitive.

The *why* of this business was articulated in everything we did, from how we answered the phones, to how we handled complaints and how everyone performed their tasks in service to our customers and the gardens we cared for. Our passion for the company, which felt like ours, the work which everyone could see, and our respect for each other and what we were doing were evident. It fueled our marketing efforts, informed the sales process, and was thoroughly ingrained in our brand.

I used both positive and negative reinforcement. I was clear about expectations. I led by example, and the success that came our way was invigorating.

Within a few months, I saw that my employees were striving to attain the vision I instilled as the leader. The fact that I was able to raise prices and profit margins while quadrupling revenue made it imperative that everyone become passionate about what we were doing--everyone from suppliers to shareholders, from employees to customers. We were all on the same page.

We started the operations analysis in December, and by January of the next year we had quadrupled revenues. After two years, we were the strongest competitor in the area.

We were getting every large commercial job we bid on and winning most of the residential work we competed on as well.

Experiential Branding: The advantage of having a brand that your employees are connected to and that runs through your company is that you'll attract new hires who resonate with the spirit and values of your brand.

Once we started to see progress and began to grow the business, it was time to develop a position that reported to me on all of the landscape maintenance work—a landscape maintenance division manager. This position entailed complete control and accountability for the division. There was no one on staff that I felt could handle it, so I advertised the position on the Internet.

One of the things I enjoyed about interviewing for this assignment was that I got to meet people from all over the world. Richard, the man I interviewed for the position was from Guyana, a place I had never heard of, let alone met anyone from. He met my criteria for hiring. He was intelligent and had a great attitude, which allowed him to be open to taking suggestions from others on the team about matters outside his skill set, like water dispersion to lawns and landscapes.

Richard exceeded my expectations. He caught our vision and ran with it.

One of the beautiful things about systems and heart is that people get it. They relate right away to the heart part of your systems.

Richard had passion, intelligence, and system experience. In addition, his strengths complemented my own, because he was skilled in areas where I wasn't. My expertise was in leadership and sales, while his was in operations. He was way better than I had hoped for.

I also hired another manager. Taylor came to us from a US national lawn and landscape maintenance company that, at the time, was leading the industry. He was experienced in managing people and systems.

Taylor was a quick thinker, a little bit impetuous, and very passionate about his job. He challenged me, and everyone he worked with, but he was open to new ways of thinking and doing things. He brought to the job systems for landscape maintenance that had been proven across the United States. We learned a lot from him and he from us. I took what he knew in terms of systems for maintenance production work and applied them to landscape installation work.

He related to the heart in what we were doing. He got it, because he operated in his personal life from the same place. People long for that in corporate life, I think. National landscape companies aren't unlike big corporations in any business.

They're usually very strong on systems, protocols, and procedures but short on creativity and heart. Taylor blossomed in our small business, run with and from the heart.

There's no reason why large corporations can't operate with the same principles we did. They just don't.

CHAPTER 14
WE LOVE GARDENING, AND IT SHOWS!

Mountain View wasn't a tropical oasis. The soil was either sandy, porous, and barren of nutrients, or it was mucky with poor drainage. Whatever the condition of the soil, growing plants in it was tough. Add on to that the area flooded with ocean water. A lot. If the salty spray on windy days didn't dry out and kill plants, the fairly frequent storms that blew through, flooding gardens with ocean water, would finish the job. Most of the people who paid for gardening services lived on the water. They knew how hard it was to have a nice garden under these conditions.

So we learned the science of maintaining a landscape with the bad soil, salty soil, and the seas that could overrun almost any garden at times. We based our methods on horticultural science and executed them with a passion for gardening and our strongest of desires to be the best.

Because we were dealing with extremely wealthy people, price was an issue, especially on landscape maintenance. Wealthy people have choices and they're extremely sensitive to price. Furthermore, our customers were experts in their chosen fields, and they wanted experts advising and working in their gardens. Developing a specialized knowledge of how to maintain gardens in this environment helped in production. We got the results we were looking for in landscape maintenance and also in the installations. Knowing the science allowed us to get the work done efficiently and at a high level of competency.

If price is no object, and you have the choice to go with a firm that offers a low price for average work or a firm that demonstrates caring, concern, empathy, and scientific knowledge in addition to passion for their work at a slightly higher price, which would you choose?

As far as Orange Blossom was concerned, I was lucky there already was a program in place and the frontline people and the managers were getting trained in the science of what we were doing;

however, oftentimes the science they were being taught wasn't absolutely correct.

Though Peter was a very smart person, he didn't really know the material, and what the managers were teaching wasn't 100-percent accurate. The subject matter has been fully researched and is available on the Internet. They would access material there, but a lot of times when they had to fill in gaps what they filled the gaps in with was incorrect.

However, the time for the crews to train was allocated and in the fixed costs. It was just a matter of teaching better-researched material. The manager involved in training was one of the people who, during my tenure, decided to move on to other things, and we were able to find someone with a background of teaching the material I felt the company needed to learn.

Experiential Branding: Developing clear sales and marketing protocols guarantees that your business will grow, even in tough times.

With a clear articulation of beliefs and company values, I formulated a sales process for Orange Blossom. Using my nine-step sales process as a template I inserted the pertinent information into it and began to sell for this company.

By following the sales process, I can average between 30 and 50 percent close rates. But after I got more familiar with the brand, I was closing during the last two years at over 70 percent. Those close rates were possible based on a combination of the strength of my process, the strength of the brand, and the close-knit nature of the target market.

Simultaneously, I was working with the managers, helping them to understand the importance of upselling their existing clients. When I first started, the upsells, if they happened at all, were because the clients demanded them, and they represented less than 5 percent of the total maintenance revenue. If total maintenance revenue was 1 million dollars, the upsells were about 50 thousand dollars each year.

My goal was to get the managers to upsell to about 30 percent on average. That would mean an additional 250 thousand dollars each year on 1 million dollars, but the company was growing.

By the time I left, maintenance revenue was 3 million dollars, and the upsells were about 20 percent, which meant we were earning an extra 600 thousand dollars each year on upsells. The improvement was phenomenal, and there's no reason to expect that they won't soon hit 30 percent upsells each year.

What ensures continued success after establishing new protocols? Active monitoring of the systems, as well as monitoring of the employees' use and adherence to the systems in order to keep the protocols vital. I had to get quite active in the leadership side of the business. It's important to assess the current situation and to create a plan for improvement.

But just as important is creating a system or platform that holds these systems, one which is easily assessable and which becomes part of the routine in doing the work. I was involved in all four areas of the business—sales, operations, finance, and leadership. As I made changes to the way they were doing things, I was also documenting the changes and creating protocols and procedures to make the systems repeatable.

I had learned a long time ago how to improve my sales through a system and have applied what I learned in that facet of business to the other three areas as well.

CHAPTER 15
MAINTAINING YOUR BRAND'S INTEGRITY

Orange Blossom had very good brand recognition, and it only got better as we grew. The logo was distinctive, and though no one really knew what the image represented, it looked very historic, artistic, and cultural in a kind of curated-museum way. Distinctive is a perfect adjective to describe it. The community it served was very small, and so the trucks were recognized and remembered. The company was big enough and had enough trucks so that it made an impression, and the distinctiveness of the logo helped people remember it even more than they otherwise would, and also made it seem like there were more trucks around than there actually were.

The other thing that was distinctive was their business model. They didn't operate out of a central location, and most of their work was billed for hourly. In this trade most of the other contractors were bidding for work based on price. This gave me an opportunity to distinguish us even further by pointing that out and explaining how our transparency allowed us to focus on doing the best job we possibly could and not focus on getting the most money out of a job by cutting corners.

Brand integrity is an obstacle for a lot of people. The drive for more and more revenue can take the heart or soul out of a business. This creates a very big opportunity for business that *are* able to maintain their vision, purpose, and meaning in their business, even as they grow. This is called brand integrity, and it can be done. Companies are doing it.

As you get bigger, there are more and more people on the frontlines, serving your customers, and brand integrity can be harder to control. But the establishment of good procedures, processes, and protocols is the start.

Having them handy to all employees is mandatory. Checklists and processes are useless if they can't be reached when needed. Monitoring systems and measuring results are imperative to having vital procedures that can grow and change as circumstances warrant. It's not enough to establish systems and procedures for doing things; they must also be monitored for their effectiveness.

It's best to have your frontline people help create the systems. Even then, protocols and procedures still need to be monitored and adapted to real-life situations as they develop. When something goes wrong and the system is properly executed, then the process may need to change. Measuring results, monitoring the systems, and ensuring process compliance will give you the data you need to judge your systems and give your people the guidance they need in using them.

Having clear lines of communication, tasks, and responsibilities has to be included in your systems-development process. Development of your company's organizational chart has also got to be included.

When I look at struggling companies, I notice that frequently a lot of the troubles they have in operations come from lack of clarity around the chains of command. Who reports to whom?

Many times companies have drawn up an org chart, but it's an out of date document that's hardly ever looked at after it's created. The org chart helps to clarify who reports to whom, but it should also be used to project labor and management needs as the company grows.

There are some countries in which it's mandatory for a business owner to submit projected employee needs over a period of time. This information is required particularly where a lot of the workforce is imported. But whether the government requires it or not, it's an excellent exercise to do as a manager or owner of a growing business.

Setting revenue thresholds, or production hours as the capacity of a position, will allow you to better understand when you're going to need more help. Using revenue or production hours as a guide to the number of people you'll need to handle the work is an excellent way to tie in sales projections to potential labor requirements.

Many businesses struggle to give their brands meaning as expressions of their core values in the market, and actually, few businesses are able to maintain integrity as they grow. Those that do will reap the rewards of being a service of value in what's assumed to be a marketplace that has been conditioned to expect low-quality offerings.

There are very few brands that people trust, especially in the services sector like electrical, plumbing, gardening, and all forms of contracting. Distrust of business runs right through the professional services as well.

I think there's a similar sentiment about salespeople. Most people aren't comfortable selling because they think they'll have to leave their integrity at the door as soon as they step into a sales position. They believe salespeople will say or promise anything to make the sale.

This could be true for some salespeople, but salespeople that sell with heart don't leave their values or integrity out of what they do. It's imbedded in their sales process and comes out in everything they promise and do. These salespeople will close way more deals than those that don't.

It's incumbent upon business owners, entrepreneurs, and marketing people to give their salespeople everything they need in order to sell with integrity. When the brand, marketing, and sales process are aligned and centered on values and purpose, it's easy for a salesperson selling with heart to create an upward spiral of success. Given a choice, who would you buy a service or an intangible from, someone you trust or someone you don't? I'd venture to say you'd be willing to pay a premium to buy from someone who you trust, especially for an intangible item or a service.

People love to buy, but they hate being sold.

Brand integrity can be systematized into your business, and it helps increase closing ratios for your salespeople. It works like a magnet. People don't just buy what you believe, they'll promote your company to their neighbors and friends. Think social media. And they'll work to help you in any way they can.

If we take this concept of brand integrity and apply it to employees, it works in much the same way. Brand integrity helps to attract the best available employees.

Employees who are invested in the brand will make the right decision when the time comes, because they'll understand the logic embedded in the brand's creation. They'll make decisions when necessary that are appropriate and correct for your business, even if it's outside of regular protocols or procedures.

If there's meaning imbued in your company's vision and mission, you'll attract people whose values resonate with that of your brand to work for your company. In much the same way that marketing attracts potential customers, marketing also attracts good employees.

When we talked about branding, we thought about values, vision, meaning and purpose. We kept the four stakeholders—customers, shareholders, the community, and employees—in mind. If you include brand integrity conceptually in the creation of the brand, all four stakeholders in your brand will be attracted to it and receive benefit.

The power of brand integrity became very clear in New England this summer, through the controversy that Market Basket's board of directors visited on their company. At the writing of this book, it's still not clear how this debacle will be resolved.

Market Basket is a family-run chain of grocery stores with outlets throughout Massachusetts, New Hampshire, and Maine. The board of directors tried to remove the CEO in a power play so they'd be able to sell the business to investors or another chain.

However, the CEO had made the brand personal. He'd taken the business to heart, and with that came respect for the four stakeholders of all the stores. When the board voted him out, employees went on strike, suppliers stopped making deliveries, and shoppers found nothing in the stores. Many shoppers, employees, and suppliers were calling talk radio stations in the Boston area, declaring their loyalty to the dismissed CEO.

It seemed the hourly employees were protected during the walk out, but middle management was not. This didn't stop managers from striking, and even after the store reopened and the board of directors threatened to replace them, many still stayed away.

I'm not sure what the outcome of all this will be. The stores have reopened, but it's still not clear what's going to ultimately come of the board of directors' desire to sell the company. The ex-CEO has offered to buy the company, and no decisions have been made at this time.

A FINAL WORD

As entrepreneurs, we each bring our unique intelligences and talents to the work we do. Each of us is different, yet our struggles are the same. When we connect to what's inside of us that longs to have an impact, to improve the lives of others, we become greater than the sum of our parts.

It isn't the easy choice to make, but those of us who do make this choice feel we're living life to the fullest and right on the edge. It's a scary, thrilling, exciting place to be, but we wouldn't have it any other way.

The green industry, specifically, and the trades in general present wonderful prospects for business owners to leverage the possibilities of the digital age in very exciting ways and to build great brands. Those who do have opportunities that wouldn't have been possible in the pre-Internet age.

I think the consolidation of companies on the national and regional levels will increase the opportunities to create well-run companies that have heart built into their systems. These companies will have a chance to grow to whatever levels they desire. We can see the consolidations happening already in the green industry and throughout all the trades as well.

Our time is now. I hope this book, if it does nothing else, allows people to realize there's a way to have integrity, passion, heart, and profits in business.

#

Bibliography

Carnegie, Dale. *How to Win Friends and Influence People.* New York: Simon and Schuster, 1936.

Collins, James C. *Good to Great.* New York: Harper Collins, 2001.

Collins, James C., and Jerry I. Porras. "Building Your Company's Vision." *Harvard Business Review* (September–October 1996): 65–77.

Gardner, Howard. *Frames of Mind: The Theory of Multiple Intelligences.* New York: Basic Books, 1983.

Gerber, Michael E. *The E-Myth Revisited.* New York: Harper Collins, 1995.

Mills, Michael. *How to Systematize Your Business* (eBook). Business Design Corporation, 2011.

Sineck, Simon. *Start With Why.* London: Penguin Books, 2009.

www.ingramcontent.com/pod-product-compliance
Lightning Source LLC
Chambersburg PA
CBHW051539170526
45165CB00002B/799